W9-AJN-239

Big Trucks

CEMENT MIXERS at Work

D. R. Addison

PowerKiDS
press
New York

For my little truck experts, Deming, Riley, and Hannah

Published in 2009 by The Rosen Publishing Group, Inc.
29 East 21st Street, New York, NY 10010

First Edition

Editor: Joanne Randolph
Book Design: Greg Tucker
Photo Research: Jessica Gerweck

Photo Credits: All photos Shutterstock.com

Library of Congress Cataloging-in-Publication Data

Addison, D. R.
  Cement mixers at work / D. R. Addison. — 1st ed.
      p. cm. — (Big trucks)
  Includes index.
    ISBN 978-1-4358-2701-1 (library binding) — ISBN 978-1-4358-3087-5 (pbk.)
ISBN 978-1-4358-3093-6 (6-pack)
  1. Concrete mixers—Juvenile literature. I. Title.
  TA439.A374 2009
  624.1'833—dc22
                                          2008021616

Manufactured in the United States of America

Contents

Have you ever seen a cement mixer at work? Here comes one now!

Cement mixers are very busy on **construction sites** every day.

Cement mixers mix cement with water and sand. The cement, water, and sand make concrete.

This cement mixer dumps out wet concrete to fix a sidewalk. Concrete becomes hard like a rock.

This cement mixer helps workers build a bridge. This is an important job!

13

The concrete is mixed in the back of the cement mixer. This part is called the **barrel** or drum.

The concrete is ready! Now the wet concrete is moved into a **loading chute**.

The concrete moves from the loading chute down another long chute. The chute is like a **slide**.

19

This worker moves the chute so the concrete is even.

Cement mixers are always ready for the next job. Great work, cement mixers!

Words to Know

barrel

construction site

loading chute

slide

Index

Web Sites

Due to the changing nature of Internet links, PowerKids Press has developed an online list of Web sites related to the subject of this book. This site is updated regularly. Please use this link to access the list:

www.powerkidslinks.com/bigt/cement/